Stock Market Gambling
Addiction Help

This book is for losers who can't stop losing their money on the stock market. If your loved one is losing money on the stock market, then this book will help them quit their gambling addiction they have with losing money on the stock market. This book teaches novices and seasoned investors about many pitfalls that may be causing you, or your loved one, to lose money if you don't know about the types of mistakes you are repeatedly making.

This book also teaches you EASY ways to ALWAYS SAFELY make profits each year. This is a short book that gives you lots of info very quickly.

Dan Plouff

About the author

Dan Plouff has a bachelor's degree. He is the author of many short books, and long books, that have to do with business, the stock market, traveling, world religions, and how to do various different things. He is also a novelist. He has taken many business classes, has over a decade of experience with the stock market, and has spent over five thousand hours researching and trading stocks, options contracts, and forex currencies.

Table of Contents

A list of some business books by Dan Plouff

- Wall Street SCAMS EXPOSED
- Stock Market Gambling Addiction Help
- Best Stocks For Calls and Puts Options Contracts
- Mad Bonds! for safe 4% a year profits on your diversified invested money
- How to Find the Best Cheap Videogames, CD's, DVD's, and Audiobooks

A list of some non-fiction books by Dan Plouff

- Surfing vs. SUP surfing
- Poker Tournament Practice

A list of some Bible translations by Dan Plouff

- Holy Bible Names Translated Version of the Book of Luke

How to support the author and this book

Please leave a book review on Amazon.com or on audible.com. Please give this book away as a gift to your friends or family members who are struggling with a gambling addiction to losing money on the stock market with a loser strategy, that is never going to work, and that is statistically likely to fail. Be sure to tell your friends and family about this book on Facebook and on YouTube. Be sure to give one or two minute long book reviews for this book on YouTube. Discuss, and debate, the topics from this book with people on Facebook and on YouTube.

If you have any questions for the author, then please ask a couple questions when you leave a book review on Amazon.com or on Audible.com, and I will be able to answer some of your questions in a future book. However, it is likely I have already answered your question in one of my existing books that you can read already.

Please send donations to the following PayPal account if this book helped you to have a lot more money than you would have had if you didn't read this book. Paypal.me/DanielPlouff Thanks for your love, encouragement, and support. Once again, that PayPal link is: Paypal.me/DanielPlouff

Introduction and legal disclaimer

This book is not advising you to do anything with real money. This book is for educational purposes only, and is only meant to be used in connection with a virtual trading demo account on a website like CBOE.com, in order to give people a basic understanding of how to quadruple their virtual trading demo account money in under a month. If you are a new trader, then you are likely to lose all of your money instantly if you lack the thousands of hours of practice, the intelligence, and the market research required in order to be a profitable options contracts trader.

This book is only for educational purposes. Nothing will definitely happen in your life, and profits are not guaranteed. This book is not responsible for any injuries, deaths, financial losses, or property damages. Seek professional, financial, medical, psychiatric, and legal advice before you ever do anything in life.

Chapter 1: Stock market odds

"Stock Market Gambling Addiction Help" by Dan Plouff. This book is for losers who can't stop losing their money on the stock market. If your loved one is losing money on the stock market, then this book will help them quit their gambling addiction they have with losing money on the stock market. This book teaches novices and seasoned investors about many pitfalls that may be causing you, or your loved one, to lose money if you don't know about the types of mistakes you are repeatedly making. This book also teaches you EASY ways to ALWAYS SAFELY make profits each year. This is a short book that gives you lots of info very quickly.

The first thing you need to analyze is if your statistical odds of success in a given stock market strategy is better, or worse, than the statistical odds of success that you have on a roulette wheel at Vegas. Many people think that losing money on the stock market is ok, but still have a mentality of thinking that losing money at Vegas is reckless and wasteful.

However, this is not true. Losing money is losing money, and there are many BAD stock market strategies that are far less likely to succeed than putting your money on black on the roulette wheel at Vegas while betting 25% of the total chips you have 40 times in a row on the exact same color on the wheel every single time.

You have a close to 50% chance of winning on the roulette wheel each spin when you bet just on black. If black comes up more often than red in your 40 spins, and if the 0's don't come up, then you are likely to have a profit. The more you play the roulette wheel, the more the statistical odds shift away from you being likely to make a profit, towards the odds being in favor of the casino taking your money.

Statistically speaking, the best odds of success on the roulette wheel come from spinning the wheel just once with all your money on one color, like red or black. However, this is a very nerve racking way to gamble. But, this is exactly what you are doing with the stock market. At any moment the market can crash, and all your chips on the table can be lost.

Therefore, it is important to NEVER put more chips on the roulette wheel, or in the stock market, than what you are willing to LOSE in a sudden terrorist-attack-driven stock market crash without being stressed out, terrified, homeless, broke, or financially destitute.

Chapter 2: The dangers of stop loss orders and stop limit loss orders

Your stop losses can be triggered at very low stock market prices if the stock GAPS down beneath where your stop limit loss, or hard stop loss, is placed. This means that if the stock suddenly crashes 75% down overnight from a terrorist attack making investors and traders panic, then if you have a stop loss, then you can get stopped out at a 75% loss, since the stock can GAP down beneath your stop loss order in order to stop you out at an enormous loss. Even if the stock does go up again a few hours later, you still got stopped out at a 75% loss, and you don't get any of the upwards bounce back up in the stock, because you were reckless enough to use a stop loss order.

A stop loss order is actually a LOCK IN LOSSES order, or a STOP PROFITS AND BE CERTAIN TO LOSE MONEY ORDER. This is one of the reasons why I don't like stop loss orders, and find them to be very dangerous. I don't think you should EVER put more money into the stock market than what you are willing to comfortably lose without freaking out in horror. Many people lose money in the stock market because they PANIC and sell.

When you buy a stock the safest thing you can do is to buy and hold it for at least five years or more. It is best if you just put an amount of money into the stocks that you aren't worried about losing, and that you don't have to bother to look at more than once a year. Oftentimes you can make more than ten times your money in the stock market in the next twenty to forty years of your life. If it is a good company that is growing, and is getting better with time, then the good earning dates are likely to be the dates that the stock will shoot up on suddenly.

But sometimes the earnings will disappoint some people, which will suddenly make the stock crash up to fifty percent down or more suddenly in one day. Many people try to use options contracts to bet on earnings dates but this usually doesn't work. This is due to the fact that the option prices usually get hiked up before the earnings dates. Then after the earnings date, the option contract prices oftentimes drop up to fifty percent or more down suddenly.

Therefore, it is actually safer to write a COVERED option contract on a stock you own before an earnings date. You can then buy back the option contract that you wrote on the stock after the earnings date. When you write an option contract you are selling an option contract in the sense that you are giving the rights to the one hundred shares of a stock you own at a fixed price to someone who is buying the option contract. You are giving them the rights to buy the stock at a fixed price from you. Therefore, it is much safer to write a covered option contract.

Chapter 3: The dangers of uncovered naked option contracts

If you write an uncovered option contract then you can theoretically lose an infinite amount of money. The stock market is never certain. Therefore, you should never trade an uncovered option contract. This is since you never want to lose an infinite amount of money. You never want to put your credit card on a roulette wheel at Vegas, while letting the casino charge a random amount to the credit card before the roulette wheel spins and lands on red or black.

Chapter 4: The dangers of day trading

The mass-majority of day-traders lose their money on the stock market. The more you trade, the more you spin the roulette wheel at Vegas. The commission costs also eat you alive. The more you trade on the stock market, or the more times you spin the roulette wheel, the greater the odds are that you will buy or trade at the WRONG times, which will lose you money in a market that is chaotic, volatile, and seemingly random at times.

Therefore, you are reducing your odds of success the more often you make trades on the market. The big swings up and down in the market are the most profitable, and financially devastating, moments in the market. You probably will miss the big swings up, and will catch lots of crashes down in the market, the more you trade, which causes you to buy high, and sell low, and consistently lose money, the more you make trades on the market. MORE people make money at Vegas, than at day trading on the stock market. Furthermore, MUCH MORE people make a lot of money at Vegas, than at day trading on the stock market.

Therefore, you are better off having fun playing the roulette wheel at Vegas, than at day trading on the stock market. The stock market requires a lot more work, a lot more research, a lot more losses, and a lot more money getting risked on the market at any given moment in many cases.

The mass-majority of people who are traders, instead of stock investors, lose their money on the stock market. A much higher percentage of stock traders of any kind lose much more money much more often than stock investors do. People who invest in mutual funds lose money less frequently than stock market investors do.

Chapter 5: The safest bonds to put your money into

One of the safer places to put your money is in the bank. However, if bank returns, and if CD returns, are not very high, then you may want to consider investing in a few AAA (triple "A" / 3A / A3) rated bonds from several different state governments and corporations. You can make somewhere between 2%-6% interest on your money in AAA rated government bonds and AAA rated corporate bonds. No AAA rated government bonds that I know of have ever gone bankrupt, ever. A very tiny percentage of AAA rated corporate bonds have ever gone bankrupt. The percentage of corporate bonds that have gone bankrupt is a fraction of one percent of them that have gone bankrupt.

Therefore, it is safest to put your money into a couple different government bonds, and corporate bonds, that are AAA rated, in order to get a decent percentage return on your money, if you want to be the safest investor possible.

Chapter 6: The dangers of penny stocks

Close to 97% of all penny stocks go bankrupt, or lose investors lots of money. These are the stocks that are not listed on the major exchanges but that are instead listed on pink sheets or on otcbbstocks.net. These types of stocks are portrayed in movies like "The Wolf of Wall Street" and "Boiler Room."

Mafias, swindlers, snake oil salesmen, and other con artists will oftentimes mail you newsletters of "hot penny stocks" that are oftentimes involved in pump and dump schemes that suddenly collapse and lose you most of your money. Occasionally these stocks leap up thousands of percent in stock price. But usually with a volume that is so low that it only leapt up in stock price because just one guy put his money into the stock. Which drove the stock up just because that one sucker pushed the buy button. This is before he then lost nearly all of his money since there are virtually no other buyers of the stock other than you who is the one driving the low volume stock price higher.

There are two sure fire ways to make money in penny stocks. Either you have to be one of these shady swindlers who is riding a thin line next to being put in jail or prison, or you can get rich through a more legal method that some millionaires have used to get rich. This more legal method of consistently getting money in penny stocks involves SHORTING the penny stocks in order to bet that the stocks will go DOWN in value. Even though you have a 97% chance that you will make steady profits by betting that the stock price will collapse, this is still not a safe investment strategy if the VOLUME is too LOW.

If the volume on the stock is too low, then you may not be able to cover your shorts, and you still are likely to lose a lot of money. While shorting a stock you can theoretically lose an infinite amount of money.

Shorting penny stocks is one of the only ways in which you can ACTUALLY lose that theoretical infinite amount of money by shorting the penny stock with low market volume. So you need to be careful. There are people who have made millions of dollars shorting penny stocks, but the best way to go is to put your money into a penny stock shorting fund, so that the risk is put onto the shoulders of the guy who is running the fund that shorts penny stocks. This way this guy will be the one losing the theoretical infinite amount of money.

This is better than YOU losing the theoretical infinite amount of money. The fund owner who is running the fund probably knows a lot more about market volumes, and how to successfully short penny stocks, than you do. You therefore can only lose the amount of money you put into the fund run by the fund owner who is shorting penny stocks. Be sure to not give him more money than you are ok with losing. Do your research. Be sure the guy is legitimate and credible. If he is legitimate and credible, then it is possible that you can earn a 1,000% return on your money in a single year, as has been done by many fund owners in the field of shorting nearly bankrupt struggling penny stock companies.

Most penny stocks crash down in price, or go bankrupt, which means that you have the statistical odds on your side. And if you are simply investing in a penny stock shorting fund, then you are limiting your market risk, by making it so that you can't lose the theoretical infinite amount of money if the stock keeps rising in price while you have a short on the stock that is betting that the stock price will crash. If the stock price keeps rising, up to a theoretical 1,000% stock price increase, or more, then you just lost over 10x's your money on that trade.

Stocks can jump OVER or UNDER your stop losses, that don't always trigger where they are supposed to on penny stocks, so stop losses are a false sense of security that oftentimes won't protect you at all.

Another problem with shorting penny stocks is that you need more capital to be able to do it yourself, and you are typically only allowed to invest a very small percentage of your money into penny stock shorts at any given time. The reason for this in trading platforms is due to the fact that the stock prices on penny stocks are more volatile. Which means that the stock price can rise suddenly, and can cause your stop losses to trigger. Which will make you lose all the money on your trade rather rapidly.

The trading platforms don't want you to lose more money than you have. Therefore, it is not uncommon for them to only want you to invest like a fourth of the capital you have with them in a short on a penny stock on the OTC or the pink sheets. Only certain trading platforms and brokers will let you short penny stocks, and most people can't figure out how to do it.

Furthermore, you also have to have a successful stock shorting strategy in place, in order to understand WHEN to short the lousy stocks on the penny stock exchanges.

It is typically best to short a penny stock after it rose hundreds or thousands of percent upwards, even though the accounting statements for the stock show that the stock is nearly bankrupt, while there are no news articles on the internet about the stock doing anything good at all whatsoever. This situation indicates that the stock price has probably risen in a pump and dump scheme.

The stock probably rose because Mafias, swindlers, con artists, and snake oil salesmen pumped up the price of the stock by mailing out their "hot stock picks" to suckers who bought the stock, similar to the "Wolf of Wall Street" movie, and then the people who owned the stock before it shot up will sell massive amounts of stock shares they "dump" on the market.

If you short the stock while it is just beginning to crash, then you can oftentimes make the same money that the illegal swindlers are making, while you are instead legally performing a completely legitimate trade by betting that the stock will crash down in value. Many people have made millions of dollars using this strategy, but there are many very dangerous pitfalls, and it is similar to betting at roulette at Vegas.

If you play for too long then eventually you are likely to lose, and horrifically. But if you want to know the best scheme you can come up with to become a millionaire with a tiny amount of money in under a year, then this is probably the most statistically probable method concerning your likelihood to succeed.

It is true that some people have turned options contracts on large corporations into millions of dollars while starting with tiny amounts of money, of less than ten thousand dollars or so. But there aren't many of these people AT ALL.

More people probably have become millionaires at Vegas than at options contracts while starting with less than ten thousand dollars in under a year. You shouldn't be frustrating yourself with gambling on the stock market, with a LOSER strategy, rather than starting your own lucrative business.

You could be spending time with your family, or could be starting a business, or could be inventing something, or could be writing a book, or could be writing the computer program to a video game, or could be going to college to get a degree in your free time. Don't waste your time with a LOSER stock market strategy that has worse odds of success than betting on a roulette wheel at Vegas.

Even playing in poker tournaments gives you a better chance of success than day trading on the stock market. At least you can bluff the other players while playing in a poker tournament, and at least you can only lose the $100 buy in that you paid to play at the beginning of the poker tournament, and at least you will have a lot more fun. You even get free alcohol at many casinos, so the casino really does appear to be more pleasurable, less painful, and more profitable than day trading on the stock market.

I am not advocating that you gamble at a casino either. But at least you have better odds of success than at day trading. You need $25,000+ to be able to buy and sell the same security in the same day repeatedly as a pattern day trader. This law was invented since it is so statistically probable that you will lose your money while day trading on the stock market. And the government didn't want impoverished people to lose their hard earned money gambling on day trading on the stock market.

The risks involved in options contracts are very unique. Options contracts have the same qualities as penny stocks when it comes to some similar issues, like the market volume in the contract itself. If there aren't many option contracts on the stock you are buying, then the spread between the price the buyers are posting, and the price the sellers are posting, can be very high.

Therefore, if you buy and sell the option contract right away, then you can lose lots of money instantaneously if there is a large spread between the price buyers are willing to pay, and the price that sellers are willing to sell at. Therefore, it is important as a rule of thumb to never buy an option contract on a stock that has a market cap of less than 10 billion dollars or so, which is a setting that can be set on stock screener search engines for stocks.

Chapter 7: Stock screeners and virtual trading

Good stock screener search engines include websites like finviz.com. I personally don't want to trade option contracts on stocks other than the largest stocks. I have quadrupled the total money in my virtual options trading accounts many times in under a month. However, I have also lost most of the money in my virtual option contract accounts many times while doing market research in order to find good option trading strategies for the stock market. I have traded real many in options contracts many times as well.

But I trade monopoly money, in option trading practice accounts, oftentimes called "virtual trading accounts" on many websites, since I don't have to risk actual money in order to see if an option contract trading strategy works or not.

A virtual trading account is virtually the exact same thing as actually investing in the stock market, or trading on the stock market, with actual money, except you are using videogame monopoly money, and aren't using real money. Slight variations in market volume may be a factor, but as long as you are trading very liquid option contracts, on very large stocks that have very high market caps, then this should be less of a factor.

I would advise you to NEVER put real money in options contracts until you have successfully turned a profit for more than five years in a row in a virtual trading options demo account on a website like CBOE.com. Most people don't become successful in options contracts concerning gaining the ability to earn incredibly high returns on their money each year until they have been practicing for thousands of hours for one to two decades of their lives.

Many people are never successful at options contracts. They have many challenges. Therefore, it is best to ONLY virtually trade, with fake monopoly practice money, on a virtual trading account, such as the ones on CBOE.com, before you begin to use REAL money.

Don't ever let anyone you care about use REAL money in options contracts until they have successfully turned a profit in options contracts on their virtual trading account on a website like CBOE.com for at least two to five years or more of nonstop success.

There should be no hurry to lose your hard earned money gambled away on options contracts that have so many different types of peculiar challenges involved with them, so much so that I can't even think of all the problems that can possibly come up, since there are so many hundreds of different types of complex horrible problems that can arise while buying options. There are many books by many authors that describe options contracts in detail, concerning how they work exactly, and so forth.

However, I am here instead to advise you concerning the statistical odds of being able to return large returns with them, without spending thousands of hours practicing with them, for many years.

The statistical odds of successfully trading options contracts without making any mistakes without practicing, doing lots of research, and being incredibly intelligent, is nearly nonexistent. You are much more likely to make money at Vegas, than at options contracts, if you are lazy, don't spend thousands of hours practicing in virtual trading demo accounts, don't understand how the market works, and don't understand how the unique trading tool of options contracts work.

In other words, I am saying to either give up now, or to invest thousands of hours and many years of your life into studying, researching, and practicing on virtual demo accounts that help you understand how you can possibly make money with options contracts.

The safest way to trade options contracts is not to buy an option in order to bet that the stock will go up or down. Instead the safest option contract strategy is to own a stock that you aren't planning on selling the stock shares of. Then, if you want to make a little extra money, then you can write an option contract on the stock between the dates that earning dates occur on if you don't want to lose your shares of the stock, or potential large profits that you could make on earnings dates by owning a stock rather than writing a stock option which could cause you to miss out on the profits.

Many people prefer to write puts, then if the stock crashes, then the person who bought the put will take the stock you own, in a complex trading situation, which involves stocks being shorted to be bought back at a lower value, that they are given the rights to a hundred shares of, through the put option, that you wrote an option contract for. If you don't understand how something works, then don't do it. If you need help or more education, then get help and more education.

Writing put options tends to be the most profitable option contract strategy, and the most consistently profitable option contract strategy, that can yield over 15-20%+ returns each year on your money. If you double your money every five years then this is a significant amount of money.

The key is to make consistent, safe, continuous, and unstoppable returns that don't stop happening. If you aren't making money in your virtual trading demo account, then don't start using real money until you can make money in your CBOE.com virtual trading demo account for at least two to five years of nonstop profits.

Trading stocks and options contracts is like playing a complicated irritating and frustrating videogame that you will probably either usually lose at, or will usually make only small profits at, as a half decent trader, who is not exceptionally successful with overwhelmingly large profits of any kind at all.

The stock market is a lot like fishing. There are a lot of big fish stories out there about a big fish that someone heard of someone catching this one time. The fish was typically smaller than the story of the fish was.

Chapter 8: Comparing stock market odds to casino odds

Many gamblers talk to you about the money they made at the casino this one time. But if they don't have a multi-million dollar mansion, then the casino probably didn't pay off for them, and neither did the stock market. This is what the stock market is. The fish is usually smaller than the story about the fish. The stock market is like fishing stories. The stock market is greatly exaggerated, just like how gamblers exaggerate the amount of money they made at the casino this one time, before they lost a bunch of money a few days later at the casino.

You have to look at the stock market in comparison to a casino. A lot of stock market strategies suck, and lose people money more often than people lose money with many slot machine strategies. If you go and push the slot machine button just once, with just one dollar in the machine, then you are less likely to lose a bunch of money, than a guy who has twenty thousand dollars in a stock that can crash fifty percent down from a bad earnings date, from a terrorist attack, or from some other unforeseen market event, at any moment.

Be sure to never put more money on a roulette wheel at a casino, than the amount of money that you don't mind losing, while still being happy, while still having fun, and while not caring that you lost that little bit of money.

If you don't care if you are forced to sell your shares of stock to the person who is buying the option contract you are writing on the stocks you own, then if you write the option contract the week before the stock has its earnings date, then the option contract will drop in value drastically a couple days after the earnings date, usually.

If you wrote the option contract, then YOU want the option contract value to go DOWN so that you can buy back the option contract at a lower value to cover the option contract you wrote, which closes out your trade, and locks in your profits.

Stock options oftentimes sell at a premium before earnings dates, and are oftentimes then sold for less money after an earnings date, since a potentially volatile event is approaching. And then you can buy to cover the option contract you wrote after the earnings date a few days later, and you nearly instantly made a 50% profit or so on the options contracts you wrote right before each earnings date.

This is another strategy you can employ instead of hoping to make money on a stock rising in value. Many stocks that have very high market caps, that are very big companies, oftentimes don't crash, or go up, a whole lot on their earnings dates, or on any other dates, ever.

Therefore, if you check the charts, and see that the stock has never moved a lot on an earnings date before, or not very often, then you have good statistical odds of being able to consistently make money by writing covered calls on stocks. But this is only if you own enough shares in order to cover your calls, or covered puts, even if the stock moves a large amount.

Remember, safety first! Never run around naked, especially concerning writing naked calls, or naked puts, in the options contracts market.

Trading options contracts is very similar to trading stocks. Except options contracts expire at a certain date and become worthless if the stock price is not higher than the strike price in the case of calls, or lower than the strike price in the case of put options. Therefore, the value of the option contract decreases simply if more time goes by while the stock price isn't moving at all. If you buy out of the money calls, or out of the money puts, then this is the way to lose the most money the fastest.

The statistical odds are that you will lose a lot of money very fast if you buy options contracts that are out of the money. You have better odds of making money on a roulette wheel, than on out of the money call options, or on out of the money put options. You are gambling, and the odds are not in your favor at all.

The safest way to buy a call option, or a put option, if you insist on buying one instead of writing one, is to buy a call option that is significantly in the money, or a put option that is significantly in the money, that has at least two months of time on it or so. There is no sure fire way to make money by buying calls, or by buying puts. You are, after all, gambling on one of the most risky forms of speculation.

That being said, if you know that a terrorist attack is going to happen tomorrow, then you can make a lot of money if you place put options betting that stocks will crash. You can also make millions of dollars if you are insider trading, and know that a stock is about to have a FANTASTIC earnings date tomorrow!

Chapter 9: The potential profits of options contracts and slot machines

If the stock price rises up $20 a share tomorrow, and if you bought the option contract for $1 an option contract, then you just made twenty times your money overnight. If you put a hundred thousand dollars into those option contracts, then you just made over two million dollars overnight. Insider trading is probably the easiest way to become a millionaire overnight, but it is very risky. Why risk going to prison for decades while risking losing all your money if your insider trading information is inaccurate?

Also, there is no such thing as a legitimate job where you transfer other peoples' money through your account to someone else somewhere else in the world. This is money laundering and will also get you sent to prison.

Many movies from Hollywood have been made about terrorists committing terrorist attacks, or that were about terrorists attempting to commit terrorist attacks, while the terrorists were putting large put option bets on the market in these movies. This is so that they could make 20 times their money in profits, or 50 times their money in profits, if the market suddenly crashed from their terrorist attack. The families of the terrorists who performed the 9-11 terrorist attacks could have turned 20 million dollars into over five hundred million dollars overnight if they placed large put option bets on stocks the day before the terrorist attack happened.

If you think an asteroid is going to impact the Earth, then this is another potentially profitable situation. If you KNOW a nuclear bomb is going to go off at a certain date, or if you KNOW an Earthquake will level Los Angeles on a certain date, or if you KNOW that some other seemingly unforeseeable event will happen on a certain date, then you can make a lot of money from put options contracts that make money if the stock price goes DOWN.

Another event that is happening more frequently, is terrorists are hacking twitter, and other social networking sites, in order to make it look like terrorist attacks happened, or that feed people false information, so that they will panic and sell a stock before its stock price crashes or crashes anymore.

It can take hours before investors realize that the news stories are bogus made up lies invented by hackers, and the company may be perfectly fine, and the news story may be a lie that the hacker terrorist made up, in order to make the stock price crash by making people like you panic and sell so that their put options will make money from the stock price going DOWN.

These scenarios are very intriguing. Understanding how they work makes the book you are reading now worth reading simply because of how interesting these scenarios are. They are interesting simply in order to think about how fascinating they are.

If you break the law then it is very likely that you are going to get caught for insider trading, or for committing terrorist attacks, and you can go to prison for a long time, just like how you get in trouble if you cheat at a casino, or in a gambling facility facilitated by a gang in a basement of a crack addict with a gun. You don't want to put yourself in danger if you don't have to, especially not concerning danger of prison. If you are going to get involved in insider trading, then it is best to do so if you live in a country where there is no functioning police system that cares enough to bother to put you into a prison in that third world nation.

However, if you are going to go through all this effort in order to make millions of dollars, then you might as well start your own gambling casino online in some third world country that legalizes all forms of gambling businesses.

It is always best to NEVER do anything illegal, or that even might be illegal. You don't want to put yourself in danger of prison, the same as how you don't want to lose your money on the stock market, or at a casino.

Chapter 10: Why losers lose

People lose money at the stock market for the same reason that gangsters lose money as drug dealers. Eventually the police arrest you and take away all of your drug money and throw you in prison. Unforeseen disasters eventually happen. Then you are doomed to work at minimum wage jobs, or to wander the streets homeless, or to start your own business doing or creating something that is profitable if you are lucky.

Gambling on the stock market is a serious addiction. It can be more financially devastating to peoples' lives than being addicted to crack, meth, cocaine, and diseased prostitutes. If your husband, dad, mom, or other loved one was sleeping with five diseased prostitutes a day, was fifty thousand dollars in debt, lost all their teeth, was living in a dumpster, lost their kids, was divorced, and was suicidal, because they lost all their money on their addictions like the stock market, then wouldn't you want to help them with their ADDICTION problems?

The same issue concerning drugs and diseased prostitutes is true concerning your loved ones who are consistently losing money on the stock market each year. They have a serious gambling addiction problem that is ruining their life and finances, and they need help.

Get them on a virtual trading demo account on CBOE.com until they can realize that they suck at trading at the stock market, and will probably always suck at it, if they never manage to turn a consistent profit at it for more than three years in a row before using real money on the market anymore.

The fact of the matter is, that if you have a loved one who is addicted to gambling away all their money on the stock market, then you might as well shoot them in the head with a gun yourself, since they may end up getting depressed before committing suicide. People leaping out of windows because they lost all their money on the stock market is not an urban myth. It is something that actually happens.

If you love your loved one then they may need an intervention in order to keep them alive if they suck at trading stocks on the stock market, but refuse to stop losing their money each year on the stock market.

It is best to tell them that they should use a virtual trading demo account on CBOE.com, or some other website, until they consistently make profits on their account for three years without losing any money in their account at the end of each year. It is likely that they will always lose their virtual trading videogame monopoly demo account money.

As long as they aren't losing their real money then at least they are realizing how hard it is to make money day trading stocks, or options contracts, on the stock market. Something like 95-98% of traders and day traders lose their money on the stock market. Those odds are MUCH WORSE than the odds you are given at Vegas on a slot machine.

The 2-5% of day traders who actually are making money typically aren't making much money. Only the best 1% of day traders are even making a decent income at their job. The reason for this is simple. It is hard to day trade stocks without eventually encountering an unforeseen market situation that can send the stock market tanking down four percent or more in a day, or over the course of a couple of days. You can incur huge losses of losing 10-50% of your money in an instant.

Furthermore, when you are day trading, or swing trading, you usually miss out on the LARGEST UPWARDS stock moves that typically happen on earnings dates. If you were an investor then you could have gotten these large 15-30%+ upwards moves in the stock price that happen in just one day, typically on an earnings date.

Not all earnings dates are good. Sometimes stocks crash 80% down or more on a terrible earnings date. But if you diversify your stocks in high market cap stocks, or in stocks that create good products, and that have solid financial statements, that don't have much debt, that don't have horrible lawsuits against them, and that have a positive EPS that isn't a negative EPS, then this is much less likely to happen to you in a critically devastating manner.

If the stock does crash then don't panic and sell. You already lost most of your money on that stock. You might as well wait forty years for the money to possibly come back a hundred times over in potential profits by the time you retire. Never invest more than what you are willing to lose.

Chapter 11: Ways to make money outside of the stock market

It is always best to NEVER do anything illegal, or that even might be illegal. You don't want to put yourself in danger of prison, the same as how you don't want to lose your money on the stock market, or at a casino. You might as well start your own legitimate business, or might as well invent something, or might as well buy rare artifacts that people don't know are valuable from garage sales, from pawn shops, or from Amazon.com.

You can start your own business selling and buying stuff on Amazon.com right now. Just buy an item for a dollar on Craigslist, and then sell that same product for more than a dollar on Amazon.com, and you have a successful profitable company. You can then say you ran your own online internet business on your resume when you apply for jobs. That's all there is to business. You just buy something, and then sell it for more money.

Collecting rare art for a couple bucks, that people don't know is valuable, is one way to do this. If you find a Picasso at a garage sale that someone is selling for five bucks, then buy the Picasso for five bucks. Don't ask if it is really a Picasso. Just buy the Picasso. Lots of people have missed out on getting to buy a Picasso, or a rare baseball card, since they were dumb enough to ask the seller if the painting they were selling was really painted by Picasso that the guy is selling at a garage sale for five bucks. If the seller knows that they are selling the Picasso for five bucks, and that it is actually a Picasso, then they are going to stop selling the Picasso for five bucks, and they are going to raise the price of that Picasso to being for five million dollars.

There are so many different types of rare items out there that will go up in value if you collect them. This includes rare comic books, rare coins, rare signed baseball cards, rare signed books, rare signed art works, and other rare artifacts that many collectors collect.

In twenty years from now if that painter dies, then your painting will jump up in value, since there will never be another painting that will ever be done by that painter. However, if you pay too much for a painting, that was painted by some homeless loser, who no one cares about, then you got ripped off and lost your money.

So use some common sense and logic if you are going to collect artwork, or anything else, as your investment strategy, that oftentimes can be a lot more profitable than the stock market, and more profitable more consistently than the stock market is, oftentimes. After all, there is only a certain number of rare baseball cards out there, and they will probably be worth more money in forty years from now when most of the copies of those rare cards get destroyed, or lost, or something.

Don't invest more money than an amount that you don't mind losing. But there are a lot of fun things that you can collect and invest in, that people haven't thought of, and these rare artifacts, like old World War 2 memorabilia artifacts, and other artifacts, will probably be worth a lot more money in fifty years from now.

Chapter 12: Betting on a slow horse at the race track

You can bet that stocks will rise or fall by betting on buying options contracts, or puts. Buying calls or puts is a bit like betting on horses at a horse track. Sometimes the horse goes too slowly. If the stock doesn't go up high enough, in a short enough of a period of time, then you lose your bet with a call option.

Options contracts can lose you all of your money, or most of your money, in a remarkably short period of time. Some people have become millionaires betting on horses at the race track. But most people don't become millionaires by betting on horses at the race track.

The same thing is true concerning buying a call in order to bet that the stock will pass a certain stock price in a given period of time. It is much safer to just own a stock, while writing option contracts on the stock you own, the weeks before an earnings date, in order to get a little extra income each earnings date. It is better to be the casino, rather than the guy playing roulette at the casino.

The same thing is true concerning options contracts. The option contract writers are the casino. The guy playing at the slot machine is the gambler who is buying the calls or puts. There is no point in buying a put on a stock that you own stock shares of if you think it might be a stock that might crash. It is better to simply sell the stock if you think the stock might crash. It is never a bad idea to sell a stock that made you a lot of money on that you think might crash. No one ever went broke taking profits.

What is bad is to panic and sell when a stock has lost you a lot of money. If a stock has already lost you a lot of money, in a big market crash, then in ten or twenty years the stock will probably be profitable again, and you may have five or ten times your money in profits in the stock in twenty years from now. The stock market is a long term game. If you want to make money quickly at it, then you will probably end up losing a lot of money quickly at it.

Most people who make lots of money at the stock market are patient, aren't emotional, and are invested in long term investments, or have long term statistically analyzed strategies that have been proven to actually work in virtual trading demo accounts after years of practice, and thousands of hours of research. Technically, you are competing against all the other traders on the stock market.

If you are a bad trader, then you are going to lose your money to those more educated, more dedicated, and more intelligent investors. Those traders will take your money if you are ignorant, uneducated, and simply suck at trading or investing in stocks on the stock market, similar to how you get eaten alive in a poker tournament if you are a rookie.

Therefore, it is safest to put your money into the bank, into AAA rated bonds, or possibly into mutual funds concerning a smaller percentage of your money. Never put more money into the stock market other than the money that you don't mind losing. In twenty to forty years from now you could have ten to a hundred times more money than the amount of money you are starting with in your mutual funds or stocks.

Therefore, it is best to have a little money in the stock market, or in mutual funds. But like Vegas, you should never put more money on the roulette wheel than the amount of money that you are willing to lose on the roulette wheel while still feeling happy, while still having fun, and while not being financially devastated.

Chapter 13: Hot stock tips can be bombs that blow up in your face

Many hot stocks explode all of a sudden. Oftentimes the hottest stocks, that have quadrupled in value in under a year or two, will oftentimes crash more than fifty percent down in value since they are very volatile, and this market correction may be temporary, or it may not be temporary. The dot com bubble is an example of stocks that went up a lot, before going down a whole lot, without ever going back up again.

Many people ask me for hot stock tips after all of the many thousands of hours of practice I have had at analyzing thousands of stocks, and options contracts, in virtual trading demo accounts, for over a decade of my life. However, there are many hot stock picks from hell. Many hot stock tips suck.

Betting on a hot stock tip is like putting all your money on black on the roulette wheel at Vegas because a fortune teller psychic told you to since they thought you were sure to win, and instead you may end up losing all your money on the roulette wheel because the psychic was wrong. At any moment the CEO can have a heart attack. Someone could suddenly sue the company. "Accounting irregularities" can develop similar to the Enron fiasco.

You can't predict the future. You might feel safe at the roulette wheel for a while, but eventually you might take a big loss, and might get desperate to make your money back, and might start losing more and more money.

Chapter 14: Ways you are losing your money as a gambling loser

Watch the movie called "the gambler" released in 2014. You don't want to be like that guy in the movie. You could be a stock market trader, or investor, who is losing money from suddenly having big losses every once in a while. But if you are gradually having less and less money over the course of the years, then maybe you shouldn't be trading or investing in the stock market.

If you have lost money in the stock market in your life then you probably have done something wrong. If you lose money every other year then you have the same track record as a guy playing a roulette wheel at Vegas. If you aren't consistently averaging your profits upwards, then you are a loser.

It takes a lot of courage to admit you are a loser, and it takes a lot of courage to tell other losers that they are losers, in order to help them stop losing money as gamblers on the stock market, or in situations like in the movie called "the gambler" released in 2014.

Most day traders lose their money. Most people who buy penny stocks lose their money. Most people who buy pink sheets and OTC stocks lose their money. Most people who buy out of the money call options lose their money.

Most people who buy out of the money put options lose their money. Many people who have shorted stocks, or who have written naked call options, or who have written naked put options, have committed suicide, since they lost all of their money, and they sometimes have lost more money than they even had, in an instant.

This book you are reading is not a get rich quick scheme. This book is a book similar to the movie called "The Gambler" that lets you take a hard cold look at some of the BAD types of investing advice that you might have been given that might make you lose all of your money. If you had received the warnings given in this book, then you probably would have a lot more money right now. This is why the book you are reading now is important.

This book is important since if you had read this book before losing thousands and thousands of dollars at a casino, or on the stock market, then you would probably have a lot more of your hard earned cash right now.

It is important to put lots of stocks, and options contracts, in a virtual trading demo account, in order to simply watch what they do for a year. What you may find is that most option contracts you buy don't seem to be profitable since the time value problem with the options makes it so that your horse you are betting on may be running too slow, and may not cross the stock price strike price required in order to make you a profit on your stock option.

What you may find with stocks is that most of them probably won't make you an enormous sum of money by the end of the year. And what you also will probably find, is that you probably didn't make any money in your stock market virtual trading demo account, and you probably didn't make any money in your option contract virtual trading demo account either. The amount of research and understanding of the pitfalls of the stock market required in order to avoid every single different type of dangerous stock requires years, or decades, of stock market experience.

Chapter 15: The pitfalls that could be losing you money

Therefore, it is important to listen to as many audiobooks, while reading as many stock market books, as possible, in order to avoid the dangerous pitfalls that you can fall into in bad investments in the stock market. Remember, more people lose at day trading, than at casinos. Also, it is important to realize that the majority of stock market investors lose money as well, but more day traders, and traders, lose money, than long-term investors do.

This is statistically simply due to the fact that the more times you spin the roulette wheel, the greater the statistical odds are that you are going to lose money. You are going to buy and sell the stocks at the wrong times, before the stock suddenly rises right after you sold the stock, or the stock will suddenly crash an enormous amount down right after you bought it, and these large moves up you MISS the profits from, and these large crashes you encounter at random moments from unforeseen market conditions, will make you lose money.

Chapter 16: The more you gamble or day trade, the more money you lose statistically

It's the same thing with a roulette wheel. The more you gamble, or the more you trade as a day trader, the higher the statistical odds are that you will lose money. It is very hard to buy a stock at the exact right moment, or to sell a stock at the exact right moment.

Therefore, it is always more statistically likely that you will make more money by buying and holding stocks you believe will be better larger companies twenty to forty years from now when you plan on selling your stocks, or mutual funds, in order to hopefully retire. Never invest more money than an amount of money you don't mind losing.

But be sure to invest a little, or you will miss out on making ten to a hundred times your money in the stock market over the course of the next twenty to forty years of your life. Don't panic and sell. Even worse, don't panic and buy. Just put a little in, no more than an amount you don't mind losing, and hold it without looking at the stock prices for the next twenty years. Then give yourself a pleasant surprise. You'll probably have a decent profit in your stocks twenty to forty years from now.

Don't get caught up in a gambling addictive mentality with the stock market. Don't get addicted to flashing red and green numbers, of stocks rising and crashing, like a gambling addict playing a slot machine. The statistical odds are that it is more likely that you will win at a roulette wheel if you put your money on black, while only playing the roulette wheel for one spin, while not playing more money than an amount of money that you don't mind losing.

The same premise is true with the stock market. Do your research. Invest in stocks, or mutual funds, that you believe will be much larger companies in twenty years from now. Diversify your investments. Spend at least a year researching your stocks before you buy them. Don't panic and sell them if they crash suddenly from a terrorist attack, or a bad earnings date, since every stock will crash from a bad earnings date between now and twenty years from now.

However, a lot of stocks will go up ten, to a hundred times over, up in value, over the course of the next twenty years from now. Therefore, just remember, don't panic and sell! And don't panic and buy while hoping you might make more money!

You probably won't make more money by panicking and buying, and you are just increasing your odds of panicking and selling when you have more money in the stock when the stock crashes suddenly from a bad earnings date or other unforeseen market condition. Which puts you on the track towards failure, and lowers your statistical odds of success.

Chapter 17: Write off your stock market losses on your taxes

It is important that if you lose money in the stock market, then be sure to write off your losses from the stock market on your taxes for the next few years. You'll probably get back a few thousand dollars in losses in the stock market by writing your stock market, or options contract, losses off on your taxes.

Chapter 18: The benefits of this book

I hope this book has educated you concerning many of the most horrible mistakes that traders and investors can make. The worst things you can do include buying penny stocks, pink sheets stocks, or OTC stocks. If a stock is worth less than five bucks a share then you probably shouldn't buy it. Stocks that have high stock prices, and high market caps, typically got there by going up in price, and they are likely to continue going up in price, much more so than stocks with low stock prices, that have crashed down enormous amounts, because their companies suck, because they are a financial wreck, and because no one wants their products or necessarily even knows what their companies even do exactly.

If you have never heard of a company before, then this is a bad sign. If you don't like a company's products, then this is a bad sign. People buy products they want, and know what are. If you wouldn't buy a product, then why would you buy stock in a product that you don't even want? No one else will want that product if you don't want to buy that product, so why would you buy stock in a company that sells a product you don't even want to buy or use in your house?

If you like Google and its search engine, then maybe people will use that product, and maybe it will be a bigger company in forty years from now. If it is a website company you have never heard of, or is a company selling a goofy looking product that you've never bought before or even heard of, then this is a bad sign. Remember, you are trying to raise your statistical odds of success.

If a stock has a negative EPS, then this is a very bad sign. If a company is losing money on its earnings, then this is bad. A company should be making money. If a company is losing money, then why do you want to put money into something that is losing money?

Another thing to look out for is a lot of debt. Although many stocks need to get into a little debt in order to leverage their profits and expand their business operations, it is important to realize that a company should not have too much debt. Be afraid of any stock that has an enormous sum of debt that is a debt level that is greater than the percentage of debt to equity that successful large market cap companies are typically in. You don't want anything that is too dangerous. This is your hard earned money you are talking about. Just because a horse with a broken leg might give you a hundred times your money if it wins, it probably won't win on the race track if you bet on it in a horse race.

The same thing is true with crappy stocks, that have a lot of debt, or that sell a product that you have never heard of before, or that sell a product that you yourself don't want to buy. If it is a somewhat small company, like Netflix, that is creating a product you like, then maybe it will get more customers, and might go up in value. Competition is something to keep in mind. But if you put a tiny amount of money in the stock, then maybe in twenty years you might have a profit in a new lower market cap company, that might get more customers in the coming decades.

It's hard to predict the future. Coca-Cola was a successful product that people liked, and its stock price has risen a lot over the course of the last few decades. The same thing is true concerning the Wal-Mart stock price and the Apple Company's stock price.

It is best to invest in a product that you like, and that other people like, that has room to grow, from a company you have heard of before, that is a company that is already somewhat successful, and that is financially stable already.

Chapter 19: Don't bet on a dead horse

Don't bet on a horse with a broken leg at the race track just because you might get a hundred times your money if that three legged blind horse somehow manages to win the horse race while you are betting on it at the race track. That horse probably won't win the race. That horse is probably going to fall over dead or something, and it isn't going to look pretty, and you are going to feel stupid when you lose your money that you are betting on that stupid three legged blind race horse at the race track.

Chapter 20: How to profit from panic

When the stock market crashed in the year 2008 it was the people who weren't afraid to make long-term investments in safe sound corporations with solid finances, and profitable business structures, after the stock market had crashed close to 50% down in value, who made massive returns on their investments.

If you put a tiny amount of money into a company like Coca-Cola or Wal-Mart after they crash 60% down from a terrorist attack, or some other unforeseen market situation, then it is likely that you will get this tiny amount of money you are investing back, with profits, over the course of the next twenty to forty years. Don't panic and sell. Don't panic and buy. Don't put more money into the stock market than an amount of money that you don't mind losing.

Imagine buying a stock for $50 a share, which was at $100 a share three months ago. Now imagine that stock going bankrupt so that it is now worth nothing. This is what has happened to many people. You have to be ok with losing that $50 of your hard earned money, or you shouldn't be investing that $50 at all.

Now imagine buying a stock for $50 a share which was at $100 a share. Imagine the stock crashing down to $25 a share a month later. It is a 2008 stock market situation all over again. Imagine yourself selling this stock for $20 a share in panic. Now imagine watching the stock price of that stock rising to $500 a share over the course of the next 20 years. You missed out on making ten times your money. If you had $5,000 invested, then you could have had $50,000.

If the stock has lots of stock splits then the stock price might still be at $50 a share in forty years. But with all the stock splits, then on the stock chart you will see that the stock price rose over 1,000% over the course of those ten years, which is ten times your money.

A stock split is when a stock that was worth $50 a share splits into two shares of stock that are then worth $25 a share. You still have $50, but instead of having one share of stock, now you have two shares of stock that are worth $25 each. A stock split is like trading your twenty dollar bill for two ten dollar bills. You have the same amount of money, but two ten dollar bills, instead of one twenty dollar bill.

If ever the stock market has large amounts of panic in it, like the market situation in 2008, then this is about the only time in which I would advocate buying put options on stocks in order to bet that they will make large crashes down in short periods of time.

You have a very good statistical chance of making a profit if you buy put options on the worst industry that has the most panic in it during a horrifying stock market recession. You might lose all your money. But you might quadruple your money in your account in under a month.

It is, however, important to not invest your money after the stock market has been crashing for too long of a period of time. Eventually the stock market is going to start going up. And eventually the investors who are making long term investments will curve the market direction from a falling crash in a bowl shape up to a rising climb up.

When buying a put option keep in mind the cost of the put option, and the cost of the stock. Divide the stock price by the put option price. This value gives you the maximum amount of profits that you can possibly make on the put option if the stock price crashes down to a value of zero dollars. If the put option sells for $2, and if the stock price is $20, and if the strike price is $20, then the maximum amount of profits that you can possibly make is roughly ten times your money if the stock price crashes down to zero dollars. The stock price probably won't crash down to zero dollars.

If the option contract is selling for $10, and if the strike price is $20, and if the stock price is twenty dollars, then the maximum amount of profits you can possibly make is roughly double your money if the stock price crashes down to zero. It is very important that you keep the price of the option contract in mind before you ever buy an option contract. Many option contracts are overpriced to the point that they probably won't make you a profit.

Buying an overpriced option contract is like buying a piece of dog poop for a million dollars, while hoping to turn a profit on the poop by somehow managing to sell it for more money. It probably won't happen. So try not to buy an overpriced option contract.

If you want to know an easy way to make a lot of quick and easy money at options contracts, then WRITE options contracts on stocks that have illiquid volumes for options at overpriced prices to suckers. This is a sure fire way to make you money as an option contract writer. You are ripping off suckers. But, at the same time, you are supplying suckers with a product they want, which is your overpriced option contract. There is no pity for losers from those who are truly profitable in their niche of the stock market, or options contract market.

Pay attention to the prices of option contracts on the highest market cap companies that have option contracts that trade in penny increments. If an option contract trades in penny increments then it has higher market volume, typically, which means that more people are buying and selling it.

When a stock or option contract has more volume, then this means that it is less likely to be overpriced, which means it is more likely that you can potentially make a profit on it from buying it.

I personally would NEVER buy an option contract that does NOT trade in penny increments. The highest market cap stocks are the ones that have options contracts that trade in penny increments. The large multi-billion dollar hedge funds who make their billions of dollars from option contracts do so primarily with option contracts on the highest market cap stocks.

The most intelligent mathematicians, statisticians, former rocket scientists, and computer programmers in the world are working for these hedge funds and are calculating the odds of success for hedge funds. So do you really think that you are going to outsmart them with your option contract trading strategy? It is rather unlikely.

There are a lot of strategies you can make based on moving averages, exponential moving averages, candlestick formations, stock patterns on a chart, and so forth. Some of these things can be useful. There are some stock patterns that you should take notice of, like the head and shoulders stock pattern.

There are some stock patterns that statistically usually happen before a stock crashes, and there are some stock patterns that statistically usually happen before a stock goes up in value. The stock market is never for certain though. Candlestick formations can also indicate things sometimes.

I've oftentimes predicted massive moves up or down in stock prices, and have doubled or tripled my money in a couple of days using call or put options contracts on these stocks with real money, or with virtual trading demo money, hundreds of times a year. But, I have never consistently made profits for over a year without eventually messing up.

I've made over ten times my money in my option contract virtual trading demo account on a number of occasions in a couple of months. However, the same can be said concerning a lot of people who have made ten times their money at Vegas on a slot machine.

If you statistically lose on more trades than you win on, or if you occasionally have a huge loss every few months, then this can stall your profits, or can put your profits in reverse. You have to look at how much work options contracts are, and how unprofitable they are for most people. Don't you think that there are better uses of your time, which could bring you more profits, less frustration, less work, and more enjoyment, than options contracts can?

Don't be a gambler. Be a winner. Don't be addicted to gambling. Know when to quit while you are ahead. Even if you never trade an option contract, and simply decide that you should never trade an option contract after reading this book, then consider yourself lucky. You didn't trade options after reading this book rather than wasting thousands of hours of your life reading option contract books, while trading on a virtual trading demo account.

You saved yourself time and money by not trying desperately to find out how to make money with options contracts consistently every single year. You should thank me, since at least I saved you a lot of time, and a lot of your money, by writing this book for you.

You can start a business. You can go to college. You can go to the gym. You can collect something. You can work harder at your job. And you can do lots of things that are more financially profitable, less frustrating, and a whole lot more fun, than trading options contracts.

Whenever you see the stock market crashing, and if you are wondering if you should panic and sell, then just laugh and know that suckers sell when panic is flooding the news. Just be sure to never sell when the market is panicking after you've already lost a large percentage of your money in a company with good solid finances, which is only crashing because there is a lot of panic in the economy.

If you think the market is about to crash, but hasn't crashed hardly at all, then maybe you should sell. But then again, maybe you shouldn't sell.

Questioning whether or not you should sell is like wondering whether or not to put your money on red or black on a roulette wheel. In the end you aren't a psychic. If you were a psychic, then you wouldn't be wondering whether or not to put your money on red or black on the roulette wheel. It's a lot simpler to just pick a color, red or black, and to just leave 25% of your chips on that color for 30 spins of the wheel, and then if your color came up more often than the other color, then you should have a profit, as long as the 0's didn't come up 30 times in a row, which CAN happen no matter how unlikely it may be.

Some people just have bad luck. That's the fact of the stock market. While, at the same time, some bad investors who don't know anything about the stock market end up making lots of money since they buy stock in companies that sell products that people actually want, and that people are going to want a lot more of in the future within the next five, ten, and twenty years of time.

There are a lot of random unforeseen market events that happen in the stock market. This makes the stock market a bit like casino games. The more you play a slot machine, the more you will probably lose, and the same is true with day trading on the stock market. I hope you will seek gambling treatment from a psychiatrist, from your friends, from your family, or from someone if you keep losing money in the stock market.

Gambling while consistently losing money is a horrible addiction. Think about all the fun things you could have done with the money you gambled away on the stock market, or at casinos. Be sure to never gamble more money than an amount of money that you don't mind losing, and that you are happy about losing.

If you are unhappy about losing any money, then don't gamble, and don't trade stocks. You should instead put your money into AAA rated government bonds with a 3% a year return rate, or in AAA rated corporate bonds with a 6% interest rate on your money each year. Or keep your money in the bank. Or maybe put a little money in a mutual fund with a successful proven track record over the course of the years on its charts.

If you are losing money in the stock market, then research how much COMPOUNDING INTEREST you would have made if you simply put your money diversified into several different AAA rated bonds from various different government and corporate entities.

The last pitfall I am going to discuss is investing in peoples' personal businesses. Family, friends, and fools invest in someone's little business. Close to three fourths of all restaurants go bankrupt, and many of the restaurants that don't go bankrupt are not very profitable. A very high percentage of millionaires go bankrupt from making bad investments in either their own business, or in other peoples' businesses. You can get sued in court. You can injure someone with your product. Your kitchen can explode and can blow up your lead chef and you can be sued for murder, unsafe working conditions, or gross negligence or something. Poop happens. Be sure to keep this in mind no matter what business venture you are planning to get involved in.

At least in the stock market you can't lose more money than the amount of money you are investing in the stock. However, if you invest into someone's little business, as their partner, then you could get sued, and could lose your house, your car, your kids, your wife, and all the money in your bank account. You can even go to prison if your product is killing people and isn't entirely safe. If you start your own business you can get sued and can lose everything.

This is the reason why corporations got started in the first place. You can gain capital by starting a corporation from investors, and you don't have to worry about losing more money than the amount of money you have in the shares of stock you have in the company. An LLP or an LLC is another viable option for you if you are starting a company.

Before you release any product on the market try to be sure it is safe and won't kill people or get you sued. Be careful in whatever business endeavor you may journey off into. There are many dangers in the world, and even though I can't list every dangerous thing that exists in the world, I hope I have broadened your understanding of dangerous investments that you shouldn't make. Be sure to think critically. You can never listen to too many audiobooks in order to educate yourself about something.

You can never ask too many people for advice. You can never spend too much time watching stocks in a virtual trading demo account on CBOE.com before you actually use any real money in the stock market rather than using videogame monopoly demo game money on the stock market.

I hope this book benefits you by making you cautious, analytical, intelligent, and safe. I wish the best of luck to you in your life. Thank you for reading this book. I hope this book makes your life better than your life would be without this book.

Be sure to read my other books about other topics if you get the chance to do so. If you have any questions or comments about topics discussed in this book, then please post your questions in a book review on Amazon.com. I may answer your questions in a future book. Thank you for your time.

How to support the author and this book

Please leave a book review on Amazon.com or on audible.com. Please give this book away as a gift to your friends or family members who are struggling with a gambling addiction to losing money on the stock market with a loser strategy, that is never going to work, and that is statistically likely to fail. Be sure to tell your friends and family about this book on Facebook and on YouTube. Be sure to give one or two minute long book reviews for this book on YouTube. Discuss, and debate, the topics from this book with people on Facebook and on YouTube.

If you have any questions for the author, then please ask a couple questions when you leave a book review on Amazon.com or on Audible.com, and I will be able to answer some of your questions in a future book. However, it is likely I have already answered your question in one of my existing books that you can read already.

Please send donations to the following PayPal account if this book helped you to have a lot more money than you would have had if you didn't read this book. Paypal.me/DanielPlouff Thanks for your love, encouragement, and support. Once again, that PayPal link is: Paypal.me/DanielPlouff

Made in the USA
Monee, IL
02 July 2021